The Science of Weapons

by Shelley Tougas

Compass Point Books
1710 Roe Crest Drive
North Mankato, MN 56003

Managing Editor: Catherine Neitge
Designers: Tracy Davies McCabe and Heidi Thompson
Media Researcher: Svetlana Zhurkin
Library Consultant: Kathleen Baxter
Production Specialist: Danielle Ceminsky

 This book was manufactured with paper containing
at least 10 percent post-consumer waste.

Library of Congress Cataloging-in-Publication Data
Tougas, Shelley.
  The science of weapons / by Shelley Tougas.
     p. cm.—(Science of war)
  "Compass Point Books."
  Includes bibliographical references and index.
  Summary: "Describes the science concepts behind military
weapons"—Provided by publisher.
  Audience: Grades 4 to 6.
  ISBN 978-0-7565-4461-4 (library binding)
  ISBN 978-0-7565-4527-7 (paperback)
  1. Military weapons—Juvenile literature. 2. Military art and
science—Juvenile literature. I. Title. II. Series.
  UF500.T68 2012
  623.4—dc23   2011035880

Image Credits:
Defense Imagery: Frank Trevino, 35, NARA, 19, 26 (top); Getty Images: Time & Life Pictures/Eliot
Elisofon, 13; iStockphoto: Duncan Walker, 10, Justin Horrocks, 38 (front); Newscom: akg-images,
11, 22, RTR/Jose Miguel Gomez, 29; Shutterstock: Boykov, 12, Daniiel, back cover (top), Debra
Hughes, 20, ella1977, back cover (bottom), Hector Garcia Serrano, 28, Songquan Deng, 38 (back);

Contents

From Sticks to Firearms

People have fought each other since the beginning of time. They handled conflict with bare hands and muscle power. They used sticks and stones. But science has changed the way we live—and the way we fight. Soldiers today need more than strong backs and hard fists. Weapons are more complicated, more precise, and more expensive than ever before. Computers, the laws of physics, and modern labs are the foundation of the modern military arsenal. Scientists are as important to modern warfare as well-trained soldiers.

Chemists and physicists work with researchers, engineers, designers, and testing technicians to create better weapons. Today's military is more brain than brawn.

Today's military is more brain than brawn.

Guns

Firearms are the most common weapons in the military. Handguns, rifles, and machine guns are types of firearms. Until they are shot from guns, bullets are in metal tubes called cartridges.

A cartridge consists of a case, a bullet, a propellant such as gunpowder, and a primer such as an explosive cap. The cartridge is loaded into a gun's chamber, which is located just behind the barrel. Handguns called revolvers have more than one chamber, and each holds a bullet. A spring-loaded hammer is on the back side of the chamber. The shooter releases the hammer by pulling the trigger. A firing pin hits the primer, igniting it and the gunpowder. Gases expand and force the bullet through the barrel. The whole process occurs in a millisecond.

Guns shoot bullets at very high speeds. Just how fast depends on the size and shape of the bullet, and even properties of the air through which it flies. A bullet travels faster at high altitudes than one shot at sea level because the air is less dense. Bullets can zoom at rates ranging from a few hundred feet per second to several thousand feet per second. Along with Earth's gravity, air creates resistance that slows the bullet so much that it falls to the ground.

Sniper Weapons

Military sniper rifles are among the most important firearms. Snipers are highly trained soldiers who shoot with incredible precision from a great distance. Their semi-automatic rifles are called Enhanced Designated Marksman Rifles.

Scientists and engineers have made several improvements to sniper rifles. The sniper rifles weigh less than standard rifles because the sniper has to carry his or her weapon for long periods of time, along with ammunition and other supplies. Snipers often work outdoors and in all

M9

The Beretta M9 pistol is the firearm of choice for the U.S. armed forces. Accessories such as lasers, lights, and sighting mechanisms can be attached to an updated M9. The sights and lasers allow shooters to focus and aim more accurately, making the gun more effective.

M-14 sniper rifle

types of weather conditions. The rifles need to fire smoothly in sandstorms, thunderstorms, and other types of bad weather. Sniper rifles are also designed to be easier to take apart and repair in the field.

Artillery

M198 howitzer shoots a 96-pound (44-kilogram) high explosive projectile

In battle, it's safest for soldiers to be as far from enemy forces as possible. Soldiers can fire effectively at targets from far away by using artillery. This includes military weapons too big or too heavy to be considered small arms. Rocket launchers and mounted guns are examples of artillery, which is classified as heavy, medium, or light.

BOOM

Chinese scientists are thought to have invented gunpowder more than 1,000 years ago. Historians believe the invention was an accident. Alchemists were trying to invent a potion that would help people live longer. One man's mixture exploded, changing the nature of war forever.

The Science of Artillery

An important part of a military's artillery system is telling soldiers how, when, and where to fire their weapons. That information comes from the Fire Direction Center. People at the FDC use computers to study information about the air temperature, wind direction and speed, humidity level, and air density. They even consider the rotation of Earth. All these factors affect the soldiers' ability to hit their targets.

FDC target processing center

A strong wind will shift a shell's trajectory, which is the path it takes toward the target. A computer looks at the wind speed and adjusts the setting so the shell doesn't move off the line toward its target. Dense air shortens the effective range of the ammunition. Air temperature affects how fast gunpowder burns. Shells fly faster and farther during hot weather.

The FDC can also determine whether the shells will explode when they hit the target or in the air above the target. Explosions above the target scatter pieces of metal over a larger area and prevent hills, concrete, and other structures from blocking the pieces. To make this happen, scientists and others developed a radar transmitter that attaches to a shell's fuse. It detects the target and explodes at a preset height. Radar sends out electromagnetic waves of energy. When the energy hits something, it reflects back as a signal. The radar uses the return signal to determine the distance and direction of an object.

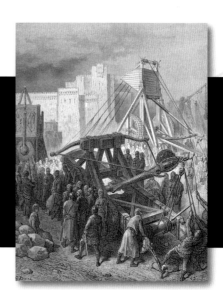

Siege weapons are examples of early artillery. They were used for long-lasting attacks in one place. The weapons flung or shot projectiles over barriers such as moats, fortresses, and castle walls. Modern artillery uses the same concept.

Siege warfare in the 1600s

Early Artillery

Today's artillery is very different from what armies used during the early history of warfare. Artillery was first used in the 1300s. A catapult is a type of early artillery. It was much like a big slingshot. The catapult threw large stones and other projectiles higher and farther than men could throw by themselves. Its main purpose was to let soldiers fire projectiles over such barriers as moats and walls, and into forts and other military posts. Catapults were used during siege warfare when an army surrounded or blockaded a town or fortress in an attempt to capture it. Siege weapons allowed armies to attack fortifications repeatedly and eventually enter them.

Stones weren't the only projectiles used in catapults. Warriors sometimes threw rotting dead animals over walls, hoping to spread disease. They also hurled burning objects to start fires and force their enemies out.

Cannons are another type of siege weapon. Scientists and engineers developed cannons that were lighter, smaller, and more accurate. The cartridge used in early cannons consisted of gunpowder in a cloth bag. Soldiers used a long stick called a rammer to push the cartridge to the bottom of the firing tube, called the bore. A serrated wire was pushed through a small vent hole in the bore. The wire was pulled to fire the cannon. The pulling created friction, which ignited the gunpowder. The resulting explosion shot a projectile, such as a cannonball, through the bore and into the air with incredible speed.

A Civil War howitzer could fire a shell more than 1,000 yards (914 meters) using a small amount of powder.

WAR

Camouflaged American artillery during World War II

Proximity Fuse

One of the most important innovations during World War II (1939–1945) was the proximity-fused artillery shell. This shell explodes near its target. Regular shells had to hit their targets to do much damage, but proximity-fused shells only had to get close. Scientists and engineers weren't sure such an explosive could be made. They knew radar could provide the right information—the height and distance from a target—but radar systems then were too large. They also couldn't withstand the forces of being shot through the air. The shell's spinning creates a centrifugal G force of 5,000. A G force of 1 is equal to the force of gravity. The G force you feel on a roller coaster—the pressure pushed against your body—is rarely higher than 4 or 5 Gs. The spinning shell creates 1,000 times as much pressure as that.

General purpose bombs line the "bomb farm" on the flight deck of the USS *Nimitz*, a supercarrier.

Bombs come in all shapes and sizes. They can be as small as a homemade pipe bomb or as large as a nuclear bomb. They can be hidden and secretly detonated or dropped from planes. What all bombs have in common is an explosion.

Bombs can consist of a metal casing filled with explosive chemicals, such as trinitrotoluene (TNT). A fuse attached to the casing ignites the chemicals. The explosion is caused when the fuse is triggered. This action can be done by a timer, by using a remote device, or by contact. A contact fuse explodes when the bomb hits a target.

Bombs can explode on the ground or in the air. A bomb exploding on the ground causes less damage because much of its force is absorbed by the ground. When a bomb explodes above ground, the burst sends energy down and sideways over a large area, causing more damage.

Smart bomb

Scientists and engineers improved military strategy when they figured out how to use electronics to guide a bomb to a particular location. Radar, satellites, and computers work together to locate a target and guide bombs to it. Called smart bombs, these weapons often save civilian lives because they hit only military targets, such as a building that stores weapons or fuel, with great accuracy. Destroying the enemy's weapons can help win a battle without injuring the people who live in the area.

Other kinds of bombs cause much greater harm than smart bombs. Incendiary bombs start fires. Armor-piercing bombs are so powerful that they can cut into the steel hull of a ship. Dirty bombs spread dangerous material that is typically radioactive over a wide area.

IMX 101

The U.S. Army is replacing TNT with a safer and more reliable explosive called Insensitive Munitions Explosive 101. IMX-101 is just as lethal as TNT but is less likely to explode if it is dropped by accident or is hit by gunfire or enemy explosives.

How Bombs Explode

A bomb explodes because of a complex chemical reaction that releases energy. Scientists call these exothermic reactions. When a combination of fuel and an oxidant, like oxygen in air, are mixed together and ignited, the fuel reacts by releasing intense heat, light, and sound. It's an explosion.

The explosion causes destruction in several ways. The initial explosion is called the blast. A violent shock wave is released during the blast. It knocks down walls, shatters glass, and smashes buildings. A small wave of energy is like the small ripples you make by dipping your foot in a pool. A shock wave is like the big ripples you make by doing a belly flop into a lake.

Smoke plume from a U.S. Army 500-pound (227-kg) bomb

The explosive shock wave can travel through almost anything. People usually think of explosions in air, but the energy and shock effect also can be highly destructive underwater or in the ground. The density of the material that carries the shock wave limits the distance traveled by the force of the explosion. That's why it's safer during an aerial bombing raid to be in an underground bunker instead of on the street.

Nuclear Bombs

Nuclear bombs—atomic bombs and hydrogen bombs—are the most powerful weapons in the world. Nuclear bombs damage a much larger area, release a tremendous amount of heat, and discharge radiation, which causes sickness and can cause cancer and death.

Other countries have tested nuclear weapons, but the United States is the only country that has used a nuclear weapon against an enemy. During World War II, U.S. scientists worked frantically to develop a nuclear weapon in order to end the war. Germany, Japan, and Italy were fighting the U.S. and its allies in Europe, parts of Africa, and the Pacific. World leaders feared that German scientists would develop an atomic weapon first.

President Franklin D. Roosevelt approved the Manhattan Project in 1941. This organization, which had some of the best scientists in the country, worked to develop the atomic bomb. In four years they were ready.

Airplanes dropped atomic bombs on the Japanese cities of Hiroshima and Nagasaki in August 1945. The bombs killed from 110,000 to 140,000 people and destroyed most of both cities.

The United States is the only country that has used a nuclear weapon against an enemy.

A mushroom cloud of smoke rose miles into the sky after an atomic bomb was dropped on Nagasaki, Japan, in August 1945.

But historians credit the use of the atomic bombs with ending World War II and saving the lives of many American and Allied soldiers. Germany had surrendered three months earlier. If the atomic bombs hadn't been dropped, the war with Japan might have stretched out for many more months. Thousands more soldiers and civilians might have been killed. The Japanese surrendered a few days after the second bomb was dropped.

Nuclear Science

One of the smallest parts of an element is an atom. People, animals, and everything else in the world are made up of atoms. Each atom contains a nucleus and electrons, which have a negative electrical charge. The nucleus contains protons, which have a positive charge, and neutrons, which are neutral. To build an atomic bomb, scientists needed to figure out how to split the nucleus of an atom, a process called fission.

Think of a group of balls placed together on a pool table. The collection of balls is like the nucleus of an atom. When a ball shot from outside the

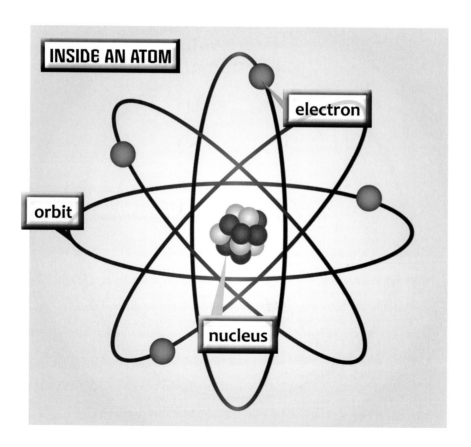

INSIDE AN ATOM

electron

orbit

nucleus

group hits those balls, they roll in all directions. That's how nuclear fission works. The split nucleus throws off protons and neutrons. In that process a tremendous amount of energy is also released.

Scientists learned that uranium has large nuclei, which are easy to split. They found that if they split one nucleus, its neutrons fly around and split another nucleus. Then those neutrons fly around and split even more nuclei. A chain reaction occurs. That chain reaction is the massive explosion of an atomic bomb. The Hiroshima bomb was equal to the force of 20,000 tons (18,000 metric tons) of TNT.

Hydrogen Bombs

Since World War II, scientists have worked on designing a nuclear bomb even more powerful than the atomic bomb—a hydrogen bomb. Instead of splitting nuclei, a hydrogen bomb is created by combining hydrogen nuclei in a process known as fusion. The nuclei of two atoms combine into a single heavier atom. That releases extremely powerful waves of energy.

Two of the most famous U.S. military scientists, Edward Teller and J. Robert Oppenheimer, disagreed about the wisdom of building a hydrogen bomb. Teller

The Hiroshima bomb was equal to the force of 20,000 tons (18,000 metric tons) of TNT.

believed the U.S. needed to learn how to make the hydrogen bomb for one of the reasons scientists rushed to develop the atomic bomb first. Americans would be in danger if the nation didn't lead in the race for a more powerful nuclear weapon.

Oppenheimer argued that a hydrogen bomb would be too big and too powerful. The bomb's circle of destruction would be so large that it would be difficult to find a target big enough to justify its use. President Harry Truman, however, sided with the scientists who wanted to learn how to make a hydrogen bomb.

By 1952 scientists were ready. A test bomb was detonated in the Marshall Islands in the South Pacific Ocean on November 1, 1952. The blast was enormous—the fireball measured 3 miles (5 kilometers) across. The entire island of Elugelab disappeared. The bomb was more than 450 times as powerful as the atomic bomb that had been dropped on Nagasaki.

THREAT

Today conflict revolves around countries that are trying to develop atomic and hydrogen bombs. Small nations such as Iran, North Korea, and Pakistan are said to be trying to develop such weapons. Because these nations are politically unstable, it is not clear how they would use nuclear weapons. So leaders across the globe hope to prevent them from getting the materials they need to build the bombs.

Testing such dangerous weapons worried many people around the world. Opponents of testing claimed that people near the test sites could become ill, and the environment could be harmed. The leaders of the United States, Great Britain, and the Soviet Union signed an agreement in 1963 to limit such testing to underground sites. Eventually more than 150 other nations agreed to abide by it.

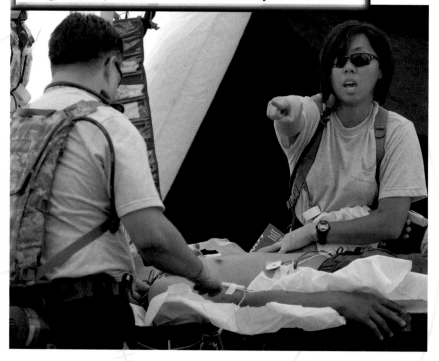

Members of the Hawaii Air National Guard assisted a "victim" during a military exercise of a simulated dirty bomb attack.

Dirty Bombs

A dirty bomb combines regular explosive material with radioactive material. When it explodes, the bomb spreads the radioactive material. Regular bombs affect a small area, so the radioactive material in dirty bombs wouldn't spread far. Such an explosion might cause mass panic, however, so military leaders are trying to prevent terrorists from getting the materials to make dirty bombs.

Grenades and Small Explosives

smoke grenades

amphibious assault vehicles

renades are small, portable bombs. The kind of explosion a grenade makes depends on which combustible it contains. Some grenades spread fire. Some release smoke. Others release tear gas. They are triggered either on impact or by a time-delay mechanism.

The first grenades were used 600 years ago. They were iron balls filled with gunpowder, weighing about 6 pounds (3 kilograms). To ignite a grenade, soldiers lit its slow-burning fuse. Only the strongest and tallest soldiers were assigned the task of grenade throwing. The heavy grenades had to be thrown at least 100 feet (30 meters) to be effective. Otherwise the explosion could hurt the thrower. Sometimes the grenades exploded too soon, injuring or killing the soldiers who threw them.

Science and engineering made a safer grenade in 1915. Engineer William Mills developed a new type of grenade. The design added a second step to the detonation process. When the grenade was in the air, a spring-loaded lever on the grenade ignited a short fuse. That delay of four to seven seconds gave the thrower just enough time to take cover before the grenade exploded.

Grenade Launchers

Grenades are dangerous because the timing has to be just right. Grenade launchers were an important invention. In World War I (1914–1918), scientists and others began developing ways to launch grenades farther than a human arm could throw them. Early launchers, such as those attached to a rifle, were more accurate than throwing them by hand. And the launchers could throw grenades much farther than the strongest arm. Today grenade launchers can be attached to

a rifle, mounted on armored vehicles, or attached to large stands in the battlefield. Some grenades are rocket-propelled. Modern grenades fly faster, farther, and with greater accuracy than early grenades. Soldiers can even program grenades to explode at a certain distance in the air. This spreads more metal fragments called shrapnel, making it difficult for the enemy to find cover.

breech

optical sight

iron sight

grenade

wooden heat shield

trigger

GRENADE LAUNCHER

Physics of Grenade Launching

Like an airplane, a rocket-propelled grenade is designed to be aerodynamic. It has a nose, two flight fins, and a tail. When the grenade is launched, the fins cause it to spin, much like a football during a pass. The spinning motion creates a centrifugal force that pushes the grenade's pins outward. The pins trigger the fuse, causing the grenade to explode.

Land Mines

Land mines are unique bombs because they don't discriminate. They are meant to take soldiers by surprise and cause injury without face-to-face combat. The person who plants the bombs can be miles away when they're triggered. But the bombs don't target just military forces. Civilians can be hurt if they unknowingly walk or drive over a hidden explosive.

Land mines are inexpensive and easy to make. They can be placed just below the surface of the ground, so they're difficult to spot. Land mines are triggered by pressure from a vehicle or a person's foot or a tripwire. When enemy soldiers are in an area filled with land mines, they are trapped.

A naval mine works almost the same way. The mines are hidden underwater. They can be triggered by direct contact with an approaching ship or submarine, by remote control, or by a sensor. They can be used to attack or protect. Naval mines that form a ring around a port provide protection for the docked ships.

Mine Safety

Opponents of land mines have urged countries to sign treaties banning their use. The problem with land mines and other military explosives is that the ones that didn't detonate during a war remain hidden long after the combat ends. The haphazard placement of land mines has killed or injured many thousands of people, even after wars have ended. In 2011 protesters cut thousands of shoes in half and placed them in a public square to represent the nearly 10,000 land mine victims injured or killed in Colombia since 1990. Land mine opponents have formed organizations to find and remove old mines and other unexploded weapons. But doing this work is costly and dangerous.

Land mine protest in Bogota, Colombia

Improvised Explosive Devices

You don't need to be a scientist to build improvised explosive devices (IEDs). These homemade bombs have five general components: a trigger, a power supply, a detonator, a charge, and a casing. The supplies can be made from everyday household items such as car batteries, cell phones, and garage door openers. To make IEDs even more destructive, nails, stones, or other hazardous objects are packed into the bombs. There are almost as many kinds of IEDs as there are people who make them.

Terrorists often use IEDs to create panic and fear. Soldiers and civilians never know which roads are safe and which are not. Is a piece of metal near the roadside trash or a bomb?

During the wars in Iraq and Afghanistan, IEDs have been the main killer of American soldiers. But scientists have developed vehicles that can withstand the explosion of an IED. Mine-resistant, ambush-protected (MRAP) vehicles are designed to deflect the force of explosions away from the vehicles.

There are almost as many kinds of IEDs as there are people who make them.

Mine-resistant, ambush-protected (MRAP) vehicle

Exploding IEDs

BURIED

Cambodia in Southeast Asia has the highest number per capita of people injured by land mines. Government officials estimate that 3 million to 5 million land mines are still buried in many parts of Cambodia. The country was the site of Vietnam War battles and a devastating civil war in the 1970s. Since then, about 63,000 Cambodians have been in accidents involving land mines and other explosive weapons. Nearly 19,000 of them have died.

5 Rockets and Missiles

Unmanned Trident missile launched from a submarine

Military rockets range in size from huge guided missiles that can fly across an entire country to small rockets that barely cross a battlefield. Larger rockets can hit planes and also reach behind enemy lines.

Rocket flight works because of the application of three laws of motion described by scientist Isaac Newton in the 1680s:

▶ **An object stays still or keeps moving until a force acts on it.**

▶ **A moving object travels in the direction in which that force pushed it. Its speed depends on the strength of the pushing force.**

▶ **Every action has an opposite action of equal strength.**

How do these three laws explain how a rocket flies? It's easy to understand that objects will stay at rest or in motion unless a force such as a push or pull acts on them. For rockets, the force comes from burning rocket fuel. That force pushes the rocket forward. The force is an unbalanced force, which means it overcomes all other forces acting on the rocket, such as gravity and air resistance.

The third law of motion comes into play next. When rocket fuel burns, exhaust is pushed out of the rocket's tail. That force has an opposite reaction, as the rocket moves in the forward direction. The mass of the exhaust forced out of the engine is much less than the mass of the rocket itself. This action involves the second law of motion, which explains how the rocket overcomes that mass difference. The more fuel that is used, and the greater the acceleration of exhaust, the greater the thrust.

ICBM

Large rockets carry a long-range guided missile called an Intercontinental Ballistic Missile. It can travel more than 3,500 miles (5,633 km).

AIM-9 Sidewinder

Smart Missiles

Scientists have improved missiles in many ways. They can locate their targets more easily than earlier models, and the missiles are more agile. New designs have made missiles that work well with sophisticated modern military aircraft.

The first smart missiles, which were developed primarily by scientist Bill McLean in 1947, detected heat from an enemy plane's exhaust. The missile locked onto the heat and flew into the aircraft, where it exploded. A prototype of the first smart missile, the AIM-9A Sidewinder, was successfully tested in 1953. Since then the Sidewinder has been improved in many ways. It now has rear-stabilizing wings, a seeker that detects infrared light, a battery for power, and a warhead that explodes when the target is near.

Patriot missile

The Patriot is one of the U.S. military's most important missiles. Planning began in 1964, when it was simply called a surface-to-air missile. It was given the name Patriot in 1976. The Patriot can detect and destroy missiles as small as 10 feet

(3 meters) long. The newest Patriot is also accurate at long distances—as far as 50 miles (80 km) away.

Human-guided Missiles

Not all missiles are fired remotely. Soldiers fire some missiles while holding them in launchers. The Stinger missile is lightweight and portable. It only needs one soldier to fire it. Soldiers use it to target enemy warplanes. The Stinger uses infrared technology to lock its sights onto an enemy plane. When the missile gets to a certain point, it automatically explodes. The Stinger is so advanced that it can recalculate its course as it flies. The range of the newest Stingers is up to 5 miles (8 km).

A torpedo is a missile fired from a ship or submarine or dropped into water from an airplane or helicopter. Like a mine, it explodes underwater. Torpedoes are closed metal tubes with an explosive, guidance technology, a detonation system, and a way to propel themselves through the water. Standard engines don't work underwater, so torpedoes use either batteries and an electric motor or engines that don't need oxygen. Standard engines pull oxygen from the air to operate. Some torpedo engines have oxidized fuel, which means the oxygen

The Stinger is so advanced that it can recalculate its course as it flies.

Torpedo and launcher
aboard a Navy destroyer

is already part of the fuel. Oxidized fuels aren't used in cars because

such fuels are heavy and explosive.

FIRE!

Torpedoes weigh 265 to 4,000 pounds (120 to 1,814 kg).
Some torpedoes are designed to carry nuclear warheads.

Weapons
of the Future

6

itally manipulated image

United States leaders want the military to be prepared to meet the challenges of the future. Scientists and engineers play a key role in making the armed forces more effective.

One weapon in development is the e-bomb. An electronic rather than an explosive bomb, it knocks out communication systems and electronic equipment by firing millions of watts of energy into the atmosphere. An electromagnetic pulse is created. Although the pulse is invisible, it's picked up by electrical equipment. The strong burst of energy destroys or disables communications equipment, including computers, radios, and telephones. Most of the technology involved in e-bombs is classified as top secret by the U.S. government.

As scientists improve this technology, they have to consider how to make it like a smart bomb so it attacks military targets. E-bomb technology now affects too many things that aren't targets. For example, e-bombs could destroy hospital equipment, computers in an elementary school, and electronic devices in people's homes.

Underwater Weapon Detectors

The most unusual weapon detectors live in the ocean. The Navy's Marine Mammal Program uses dolphins and sea lions to save lives. The fantastic swimmers can detect, locate, and mark mines. They also detect and mark enemy swimmers who pose a threat to ships and harbors.

The bottlenose dolphin and California sea lion have two special skills. First, they are strong and precise divers. Unlike humans, dolphins and sea lions can dive deep and quickly swim back to the

The Navy's Marine Mammal Program uses dolphins and sea lions to save lives.

Navy dolphin K-Dog wears a pinger device that allows it to be tracked underwater.

surface. Humans must stop for a while at certain distances as they rise from deep locations. If human divers don't take time to adjust to the changing water pressure as they move back to the surface, they can get very sick or even die.

Dolphins and sea lions also have amazing sensory skills. Even the Navy's best equipment can't compete with a dolphin's internal sonar. Dolphins use echolocation to accurately detect mines and other objects, even in deep, murky water. The sounds the dolphins make echo off objects. The dolphins listen to the echoes to find and identify the objects. Sea lions don't use echolocation, but they have keen sight and hearing, can swim through tight spaces, and can go onto shore if needed.

The Navy does not train marine mammals to hurt humans. Dolphins and sea lions are not used to carry weapons to attack ships. They are rarely hurt doing their detection work. Once they've marked a mine, they swim away to safety and humans do the work of disabling the mine.

SONAR

With its amazing sonar capabilities, a dolphin can tell the difference between a BB gun pellet and a kernel of corn from 50 feet (15 meters) away.

Unmanned Weapons

Every time a soldier enters a battle, he or she runs the risk of being injured or killed. But what if weapons didn't require someone with the weapons to fire them? Today some military vehicles are unmanned, operating by robotics.

Predator drone

They include a military drone aircraft called the Predator. The Predator is navigated by means of satellites and cameras that send information to a pilot who controls the plane remotely. The Predator was developed for spy missions, but it can also be fitted with missiles for combat missions.

The military plans to extend its unmanned weapons program in the future. Scientists are working on a combat robot known as the Gladiator, a tactical unmanned ground vehicle. The Gladiator will be armed with a machine gun and grenade launcher. The fighting robot will also be used to check out enemy land, clear mines, and remove obstacles.

Whether the United States is at peace or at war, scientists and engineers are the key to the nation's

Gladiator tactical unmanned ground vehicle with wheels

Gladiator tactical unmanned ground vehicle with tracks

progress. They research, design, and create the technology and tools that make our lives better. If the military couldn't take advantage of science, soldiers would face much more dangerous conditions. In the information age, science is America's greatest weapon.

Glossary

atom—an element in its smallest form

centrifugal force—the force that pushes a rotating object outward from the center

combustible—a substance that ignites and burns readily

echolocation—the process of using sounds and echoes to locate objects

element—a basic substance that cannot be separated into simpler substances

fortifications—buildings or walls built as military defenses

hydrogen—a colorless gas that is lighter than air and burns easily

infrared light—light that produces heat; humans cannot see infrared light

physics—the study of matter and energy, including light, heat, electricity, and motion

projectile—an object propelled through the air by a weapon

radar—a device that uses radio waves to track the location of objects

radiation—tiny particles sent out from radioactive material

satellite—a machine that circles Earth; satellites take pictures or send signals to Earth and receive signals from Earth

serrated—saw-toothed

shell—an artillery projectile containing an explosive charge; a very large bullet

sonar—a device that uses sound waves to find underwater objects

uranium—a radioactive metal that is used to generate electricity at nuclear power plants and to make nuclear weapons

Read More

Dougherty, Martin J. *Weapons and Technology*. Pleasantville, N.Y.: GS Learning Library, 2010.

Fridell, Ron. *Military Technology*. Minneapolis: Lerner Publications Co., 2008.

Harmon, Daniel E. *Chemical and Biological Weapons: Agents of War and Terror*. New York: Rosen Pub., 2009.

Parker, Steve. *Military Machines*. Broomall, Pa.: Mason Crest Publishers, 2011.

Internet Sites

Use FactHound to find Internet sites related to this book. All of the sites on FactHound have been researched by our staff.

Here's all you do:
Visit *www.facthound.com*
Type in this code: 9780756544614

Read all the books in this series:

Science of Military Vehicles
Science of Soldiers
Science of Weapons

Select Bibliography

Clear Path International
www.cpi.org

Diagram Group. *The New Weapons of the World Encyclopedia: An International Encyclopedia from 5000 B.C. to the 21st Century.* New York: St. Martin's Griffin, 2007.

E-MINE: Electronic Mine Information Network
www.mineaction.org

Exploring the History, Science, and Consequences of the Atomic Bomb
www.atomicarchive.com

Grenade Launcher History
www.grenadelauncher.com

Los Alamos National Laboratory
www.lanl.gov

Physics: The Race to Build the Atomic Bomb
www.cccoe.k12.ca.us/abomb/physics.htm

Weir, William. *50 Weapons that Changed Warfare.* Franklin Lakes, N.J.: New Page Books, 2005.

Index

About the author

Shelley Tougas is an award-winning journalist and author. This is her sixth book for young readers. Shelley lives in south-central Minnesota near the prairie home of Laura Ingalls Wilder, one of her favorite writers from childhood. Shelley and her daughter, Samantha, enjoy following and re-living the adventures of the Ingalls family.

MAY - 9 2012 #29.90